PRAISE FOR THE AUTHOR

"The juggling act of being a Christian, mother, wife, and entrepreneur can often feel impossible, but Rebekah is someone I have always admired for her ability to strike the proper faith, family, work balance. This book serves as a amazing guide for momtreprenuers looking to find a similar life rhythm."

Paul Ten Haken
CEO of Click Rain

"I've known Rebekah for many years, from a time when both of us had not much more than wide eyes and big dreams. The thing that impressed me about Rebekah both then and now is her philosophy of "wife first, mother second, umbrella of God over all."
She's worked hard for what she has and I'm so thrilled at the success she's achieved in her personal and professional life."

Melissa Johnson
Owner of Oh My Cupcakes and Oh My Word, and author of *Fingers in The Frosting*

"Working with Bekah and her team is a true honor and privilege. We've worked with hundreds of businesses and people over the past seven years and Bekah is simply one of the best. Her passion for her business is unmatched and her positive energy is truly contagious. What's most impressive is how she manages to be a razor-sharp businesswoman, friend, business partner, wife, and top-notch mom of four all at the same time. It's obvious to see how she weaves family and business together, and that's what makes her product so authentic. It's refreshing to see her company do well as proof that it's still possible to keep family and faith a priority while still managing a successful business."

Travis Rhoades
CEO of Web Concentrate

"Rebekah lives a faith-filled, full-plate, full-house, and full-throttle business lifestyle. Rebekah, like all humans who find a way to successfully navigate a path they choose to walk, and then turn around to help others on their journey, has my full respect. "If you're looking for answers, options, honesty, and some guidance, Rebekah's experience will help light the way for you to execute the life you desire."

Travis Jacobs
Author of *Rhythm Wisdom: The Endangered Humans' Traveling Guide*

"I've had a deep level of admiration and respect for Rebekah for years. As a fellow small business owner and parent of young children, I greatly appreciate her insights on how to balance the crazy life of an entrepreneur with her calling of being a parent. Can you relate? If so, I highly recommend this book."

Nathan Rueckert
Founder & Owner of The Baseball Seams Co., LLC.

EQUIPPED to EXECUTE.

EQUIPPED to EXECUTE.

Guiding Moms To Joyfully
Impact Family And Business

REBEKAH SCOTT

THRONE
PUBLISHING GROUP

Throne Publishing Group
2329 N Career Ave #215
Sioux Falls, SD 57107
ThronePG.com

DEDICATION

To my hubby who sees me fit to live this dream, to my parents coaching me to do my best above the rest, to my siblings who never let me settle for comfort, and to my team who cheers me on with each new rise in the roller coaster!

TABLE OF CONTENTS

INTRODUCTION

A mompreneur is someone who simultaneously rocks the two toughest gigs on the planet: motherhood and entrepreneurship. While other people may see chaos, a mompreneur sees the kids fed, dressed, and out the door on time—just like the orders she shipped the night before. She's the one who has processes, systems, and methods for all the madness life has to offer. And she makes it look good while doing so!

The big question is, am I describing you right now?

Before you answer that question, answer these:

- Who knows what your children need more than you do?
- Who understands what it feels like to live on no sleep, little thanks, and a never-ending list of to-dos?
- Who else gets how crazy it is that you can go from changing a dirty diaper one second to interacting with a professional customer the next?
- Who else loves your family—and your business—as much as you do and wants nothing more than to see them at their best, happiest, and most fulfilled?
- Who else has dedicated her life to them?

The answer is you.

If this book is in your hands, you are the only one who fits the job description listed above. And it just happens to be what a true mompreneur looks like.

In this book, I'm going to prove you already have everything you need to be successful. It's only a matter of time and everything will come into alignment.

Read on, and I'll show that you're already equipped to execute!

PART ONE

STARTING

1
THE ILLUSION

On a hot June day, I scrambled to pack for an art show. I flew in and out of the house, arms full of purses and product. I ran by my one-and-a-half-year-old son, Gus, who was playing by himself. My mind raced and my phone dinged with constant notifications and reminders. Each time I marched past Gus, he tugged on my leg, asking for a snack.

I kept telling him, "Just a minute. Mommy is working." Then I remembered that I still hadn't planned any meals for him and my husband while I'd be gone. Oh, and on top of that, it was Father's Day weekend. My name wasn't about to top any mom- or wife-of-the-year awards lists.

Gus tottered over yet again and tugged on my leg. But this time I lost it, and screamed out loud, "STOP!" Then it happened. His little lip quivered and his big blue eyes welled up with tears. His tears rolled down his cheeks and I knew my little boy was confused about what just happened. "What did I do wrong?" his eyes asked. I hated that I was leaving. But at this point, I see another choice.

My business was as young as my son, and I had tons of passion and desire. But I simply couldn't leave my family like this. So I made a choice. I called the organizers of the art show and backed out—which is a big, bad deal. When you cancel last minute on art shows like this, you run the risk of being blacklisted. They don't like flighty people who don't show up.

Now, I had another title to add to my resume: *failing business-woman.* I scooped up my little guy, held him in my arms, laid down on the floor with him, and sobbed. I felt like a total failure. But this became a defining moment for me. If I wanted to be the wife, mother, and business owner I knew I could be, I had to find a better way.

I began devouring every book and podcast I could find on pro-cesses, systems, and models. I knew there was a way to fulfill my role at home and run a successful business at the same time.

In the days that followed, I felt immediate relief. I was on to something. A strange calm and power materialized as I carved out my own future. I felt control placed firmly in my grip. I crafted a plan to fulfill all of my roles—and be happy while I did it. But the best part is, it worked! And today, the book you hold in your hands is the product of this pursuit.

As a mompreneur (mommy plus entrepreneur!), I've learned to blend my life and company together in a way that benefits both. To begin, however, there are many people who don't believe this can be done. In fact, there is a stereotypical image of work-from-home moms floating around in our culture. Rather than skilled entrepreneurs and moms, they're seen in a less dazzling light. In fact, if you asked most people, here's how they may describe a work-from-home mom's typical day.

A DAY IN THE LIFE OF A WORK-FROM-HOME MOM

She wakes up to an alarm clock of crying kiddos and hungry bellies. Showering is a luxury and makeup a pleasant dream. No superhero cape for her—just yesterday's yoga pants decorated with crumbs, milk splashes, and worn-out knees from chasing toddlers on carpet! (Who has time to do yoga, anyway?) She scoops up her kids, feeds them, and wrangles them into clothes that match (sort of). Then, it's time to plow through her hodgepodge of a calendar.

Her day is filled with errands, appointments, and chauffeuring car seats in a minivan. She arrives at every appointment 15 minutes late. She tumbles into the grocery store with that frizzy, fresh-from-the-battlefield look. She bumps into some family friends in the produce section who ask her, "How's that little business going?" She tries to keep from rolling her eyes, then feels the urge to prove her legitimacy once again. She doesn't *just* stay at home; she runs a real business. And all while feeding and potty training her tiny coworkers and loving her husband as best she can. What she does is actually a triumph! But she has to prove her worth as both a business owner and mom at every turn.

She didn't start a business because she was bored and needed something fun to occupy her time. However, she must admit that she isn't working a methodical plan. She's flying by the seat of her pants and hoping to keep all the seams from bursting.

During nap time, she's fielding calls and working in spurts, all the while wondering what she's going to feed everyone for supper. She knows what success looks like but has no real plan to get there. And, if she's being honest, she's actually a little scared of it. After everyone's in bed, she's back to work. It's time for more late hours before collapsing into bed, waiting for the child-powered alarm clocks to sound in just a few hours. And somehow, her Frankenstein of a to-do list is actually longer now than when the day began.

She feels unaccomplished and overwhelmed. But is this what running a business from home and being a mom at the same time looks like? If so, the real fear is that she can only be good at one or the other. This means a business that sputters and sparks but never really gets anywhere. This means the guilt of neglected kids and silent judgment from super-moms who make their own soap, volunteer for numerous committees, and and have an essential oil potion for every ailment.

They aren't fakes or frauds. They're the real deal, willing to put in long hours and late nights. But even though they mean well, they fail at prioritizing their business. They're burdened with guilt every day because they think the choice is between being a good business owner and being a good wife and mother. In their minds, it's either one or the other. They know what success looks like, but they're just not sure how to get there. So, they spin in place hoping to get unstuck.

SEEING THROUGH THE ILLUSION

As I'm writing this, I've been in business for 13 years. I've raised four kids (though it feels like five with a two-year-old) all while growing my business—Rebekah Scott Designs—into a team of 20 amazing people. But it didn't happen overnight. And there were a lot of days in my crazy, beautiful circus that were filled with no showers, food-stained yoga pants, and tears.

I've lived in the scramble. But what I've learned is that the choice between being a good mom *or* a good business owner is an illusion. It's not true. So take a deep a breath and get ready to dig your super-hero cape out of your closet.

While the struggle is real, there is a way out. There is a real path to making money while nourishing your family. There is a method for running a well-oiled business and baking home-made bread.

For me, the change was that moment where I was curled up with Gus on the floor. As we cried together, I burned the moment into my mind. I held on to it, determined never to be there again. This set me on a course of transforming from work-at-home mom to mompreneur. In this book, I'm going to share with you the steps, processes, and systems you need to put into place so you can have confidence that your business and plans are uniquely gifted from God.

It's time to kick self-doubt to the curb and think big. To do this, you need to start with a written plan based on your personal priorities; a plan you can execute with joy while keeping all of your eggs in one basket. A pretty basket filled with happy chicks and plenty of room for flight and wing expansion!

So let's take a look at what your new way of doing life and business will look like.

A TRUE MOMPRENEUR

A true mompreneur believes in her plan. She's confident in her desires and knows the right people to talk to and exactly what to ask them. She doesn't waste time trying to learn and do everything by herself. Instead, she equips herself (and makes phone calls) with advisors and mentors to help her execute the master plan. Along the way, I promise she'll also be humbled on her journey. And if she stays on this path, her dream will keep outgrowing what she continues to accomplish.

Her Thoughts

Her thoughts aren't filled with resistance. Instead of thinking, "How can little old me do that?", she hears God whisper, "Watch what I'm about to do through you. I've already equipped you to succeed and you're going to do things far larger than your dreams. Remember how much bigger than you I am!"

Her Attitude

Her attitude is positive on purpose! She makes a choice to be uplifting, excited, driven, and disciplined all at once. And she can do this every day because she's found her sweet spot of creativity and giftedness. Seriously, put me in my fabric closet for five minutes and I'll come out happy.

She's also full of hope. She can say without flinching, "I will succeed." She's filled with love. She believes, "I am doing this for my family." She has grace for the journey. She knows, "I won't always get every step right, but I will keep trying. Failure is only a change in direction along the road to realizing my dreams." She thinks outside of the box. She's made up her own mind and decided, "I know what everyone says my life *should* look like, but I'm going to pursue my own vision for what I *want* it to look like." She owns her life's vision and purpose, not anyone else.

Her Average Day

Her days don't happen to her. She happens to them. Her days are organized to execute and complete exactly what needs done to move the ball forward. She knows exactly what to do on Monday to set up an entire week of getting crazy amounts of quality work done. And guess what? There's also room for house chores, dirty diapers, and sunset conversations with her hubby. She hits all of the main areas for her priorities, takes time for self-care, for God, for family, and for work. Every important thing has its sacred place.

Her Goals

No longer do her goals flit and bounce around in her head. They're an action plan organized into daily, weekly, monthly, and yearly pieces of the big puzzle. She has concrete goals for herself, her family, and her business. And as she racks up the wins, she can lay her head down at night fulfilled. There is more joy in the day because it's well-planned and executed. Really, she's in control of her business and dream. She's not just chasing it—she's living it! She can see progress and gains momentum.

Her To-Do List

A mompreneur's to-do list is filled with actionable items directly driven by her goals. And they can still be crossed off! Her list touches upon all of her roles so she gets everything done in a beautiful (though sometimes messy), coordinated effort. For example, here's what a mompreneur's to-do list may look like:

1. Email influencer about promoting new product.
2. Call photographer to set up photo shoot.

3. Teacher conference call about kids' reading goals and school progress.
4. Listen to podcast about leadership from Pat Flynn, then email learning points to team.
5. Plan out weekend food menu for football tourney.
6. Start mission trip conversation with hubby.

Then, before she starts this magic to-do list, she reviews it. Her first step is to prioritize. She picks the top three things that must get done today. Then, if time allows, she gets gold stars for every other item she knocks out.

MY JOURNEY TO MOMPRENEUR

I get pumped up just writing about this because it describes my own journey! It's a journey I'm so passionate to help other work-from-home moms walk for themselves. As I reflect on my life, I've realized my mompreneur story has its start when I was just four years old.

My mom has always been an incredible seamstress. I loved watching her work at her cutting table. She'd sing, laugh, and sew in her happy place. It was a joy to be in that space with her. She was so in her element, it was contagious. She made denim shirts with applique and beautiful curtains. But the thing was, she barely charged anything for them. I loved seeing her work with so much joy and hearing people exclaim, "You made that?!" when seeing her creations. However, she never believed in herself or her work enough to sell it for what it was worth. She undervalued her effort and gift. So, even as a girl, I vowed to change that for myself—and, if possible, for her, too.

I learned to sew and serge from her and have carried on the time-honored tradition. And just like her, I knew I could design and sew. However, when I held my first baby, Gus, I also knew I didn't want to leave home. I wanted freedom in my day because I prize time with my babies and family over cubicles and spreadsheets. I believed I had it in me to design and create for a living. This was also my chance to build on my mom's gifts that she taught me.

My business started the way so many mompreneurs' do. I was working a run-of-the-mill, eight-to-five job and my husband, Nicholas, was working full-time as well. We worked our financial plan to pay off my school loans and got out of debt. As we did this, I sewed purses as my creative outlet. They were quick to make and I loved the confidence boost when people admired my work! I also love giving gifts. So as Christmas approached one year, I decided they would make perfect presents.

They were a hit and I immediately got orders from friends and family. Then, a stroke of insight struck—I could do this full-time and be in complete control of my day and happiness. So, once Nicholas and I were debt free, I made my big pitch. I would transition out of my eight-to-five job and work as a full-time designer. My husband threw his full support behind me and I've never looked back (although sometimes I miss regular paychecks)!

I remember my first official day of designing. I sewed from three in the afternoon to two in the morning without noticing how time had passed. I was so energized and excited that I was up and at it again by six the next day. Watching my mom work at such a high level without ever realizing the full value of her work has driven me since day one. Her creative journey helped me understand that if someone likes it, you can put a dollar amount to it! I also saw the opportunity to pursue a worthy business ideal for God's purpose and glory.

I'm humbled that I get to make a living doing what I love. Especially because it's a time-honored tradition passed down through my family. Because of this, I wanted to prove people would pay a high dollar amount for our skill and work.

My mom's story is a major part of my drive. But I also remember seeing the moms at my eight-to-five job. They dragged themselves in, tired and spent. I saw them cry in the parking lot from a mixture of bad mornings with their kiddos, sleep deprivation, and guilt at having to leave them. I also vividly recall conversations where they brandished their children's "report card of firsts" from daycare. The daycare workers saw their children take their first steps and heard their first words. They catalogued it for their mothers in black-and-white bullet points on a page.

Don't get me wrong—I've missed plenty of firsts, even working from home. My kids have taken steps without me and had plenty of other big moments beyond my eyes. But I resolved I wouldn't watch my child grow up via a spreadsheet and anecdotes. This isn't to shame anyone that does choose this route! Each of us has been gifted with a journey God has laid before us, and you should trust yourself to travel that journey. I just knew I wanted to be present for as many of those moments as possible.

My journey didn't begin with having everything together. It began with deep desire and conviction. And I bet yours began this way, too. I realize my ideals and dreams may not be the same as yours—and that's completely okay! Maybe you don't sew or sell anything. But you, just like me, can still do things better. So, I invite you to join in the pursuit of happiness and fulfillment of your God-given gifts. All I needed were some tools, processes, and systems to guide my inner fire. So let's take a deep dive into the nitty-gritty of how to grow a killer business, nurture our families, and make ourselves ever happier while we're at it.

Question 1

Why do you want to be a mompreneur?

Question 2

What would your ideal day look like working from home
(minus life circumstances like potty training and sick kids)?

Question 3

What part of being a mompreneur
are you most excited to work on?

Question 4

Are there any places you've undervalued
your skills, gifts, and abilities?

Question 5

What part of the mompreneur journey
are you excelling at right now?

2

FIRST THINGS FIRST

affectionately refer to my life as a crazy, beautiful circus because that's what it is. It's full of color, zany antics, daring feats, a whole lot of noise, and the occasional rogue animal! And I know I'm not alone. So how do you build a business, nurture a family, love your husband, and invest in yourself amidst the chaos? The answer is found in the marriage of two words: priorities and boundaries. Get to know them, because they are about to be your superhero sidekicks.

PRIORITIES AND BOUNDARIES

Priorities and boundaries are the most important metrics by which to measure your life. After I'm gone, people will know what I held important because of the fruit I produced. It will be evident by what I prioritized by my actions, not just words.

I want people to see I prioritized my marriage by adoring my husband and supporting his dreams. I want people to know I loved my family by helping my children discover their gifts through daring to do big things. I want people to recognize I valued my work by setting huge goals and accomplishing them with purpose. I also want people to remember I honored myself by serving God, who saw me fit to minister to, coach, and mentor hundreds of mompreneurs through books, conversations, and podcasts.

At their most basic level, priorities are what comprise the bulk of your hours every week. They are the roles in which you have been gifted (they're gifts, not duties!). For me, my priorities are: servant of God, wife to Nicholas, mother of four, and owner/designer of Rebekah Scott Designs. So if you look at my calendar, that's exactly what you'll see reflected.

If priorities are what drive your actions, boundaries are the framework they operate within. They function as a dynamic duo. They fuel and propel you to fulfill your purpose. Combined, they form a rough sketch of who you are as a person in each of your roles. Priorities are the bullet points, and boundaries keep you accountable and coloring inside the lines. Or, put another way, they set the framework for your dreams to thrive and be fully "colored in" as they unfold into a greater masterpiece.

For example, by setting simple boundaries for my business in the beginning, I was more equipped to say no and more confident when saying yes. All kinds of opportunities and requests cropped up. So to stay focused and make wise decisions, I needed a way to measure them. My boundaries became a measuring tool so I could keep coloring in the lines. To date, I haven't changed my whole masterpiece. I've simply made a bigger frame and added details. I started with a picture of a strong lioness, and now I've added four cubs!

THE IMPORTANCE OF PRIORITIES AND BOUNDARIES

It's hard to overstate their importance. Without set priorities and boundaries, you will spin in place. They are tracks to help you move forward. Or, think of it like this. How many times have people asked you, "How's your business going?" And how many times have you had a tough time coming up with a good answer?

Priorities and boundaries are your secret weapon here. Because you have clearly defined what you're going to pursue, you can confidently answer, "Business is great—I'm up 15 percent from last year." No lying or fluffing numbers. Instead, you can answer honestly because you have a strong grasp of what's really going on.

The dynamic duo helps you define exactly what you're aiming for. This means your business evolves from a rough napkin sketch into a painting fit to hang on a castle wall. Why? Because you've bought the frame, painted on the canvas, and know precisely which strokes of the brush to combine to bring your vision to life.

WHERE TO START

If you're a work-from-home mompreneur like me, you must set priorities and boundaries in a few key areas. Remember, you're not asking for permission from anyone here. You're setting them for yourself. You have to determine them first, because you're the only one with a clear vision for the masterpiece. Resist the urge to be a people pleaser!

Ordering Your Priorities

To start, know that how you order your priorities is important. Notice how I structured mine:

1. Servant of God.
2. Wife to Nicholas.
3. Mother of four.
4. Owner and designer of Rebekah Scott Designs.

This means I have an order of operations for my life. First things first, I'm a servant of God. This means daily devotions, prayer without ceasing, and having "two chairs" conversations (one chair is for me and a the other is for God). Next, I'm a wife. I nurture my husband with food, drink, sleep, and speaking his love language: quality time. Which honestly makes me wonder if God was playing a joke on me!

After that, I'm a mother. I want to see the majority of their firsts and have the freedom to prioritize them. I want to know what their gifts are and nurture their interests. And finally, I'm a business owner and designer. I will be a good leader to my staff of 20 and show them the same grace I require. And we're all going to use every last ounce of talent God gave us.

What do your priorities look like? You may not be a wife, mom, or business owner, but you do have important roles to prioritize. Are you a writer? Sister? Friend? Giver? Inspirer? Artist? Daughter? Whatever you are, set and order them for yourself.

Framing Your Masterpiece

Boundaries, as I've described, are the framework you work and live within. For instance, in order to be a work-from-home mom, I can't get an office, studio space, or storefront away from home. I've set that boundary and I'm not about to cross it. Another example is that I won't do 30 weekends of shows across the country each year to advance my business. However, I can pursue 30 bloggers and influencers to promote my products.

The core to setting and holding to your boundaries is overcoming fear. It's stopping the lie that if you don't give your business everything, it will crumble around you. You see, when you don't live within your frame, your life becomes owned by everyone else. You exist beneath the tyranny of other people's wants rather than experiencing the freedom of fulfillment. You'll flit from one big thing to the next, but never really get anywhere.

Remember the chaos of the stereotypical work-from-home mom in chapter one? That's what an average day looks like for people who don't set their own priorities and boundaries. This is the path for work that energizes you rather than depletes you. Here's the real deal. By taking them seriously, you're taking yourself seriously. Cue the wind machine for my awesome cape!

HOW TO SET YOUR OWN PRIORITIES AND BOUNDARIES

The first step to setting priorities for yourself is knowing your roles and listing them in order of importance. From here, you need to ask yourself two questions:

1. What does each role require of me?
2. What does success look like in each role?

Do you see how those answers begin to steer your course? However, there are some sticky spots to look out for.

For me, I had to get over an underlying guilt of prioritizing my husband over my kids. But for me, I asked the question, "Who came first: him or them?" He did, of course! So I believe it's best and healthiest for our entire family for it to stay that way.

As you prioritize them, you also need to understand what you're committing to. You see, you're not simply committing to these roles. You're setting the internal expectation that it's impossible to fulfill them all at once. While you can do them all, they can't all happen at the same time.

To help overcome these sticky spots, I learned to define what I call *deal breakers*. They are the things that, if I see happening, I know I've drifted from my priorities. Here are some examples of my deal breakers:

1. Am I neglecting knowing God intimately and following his lead?
2. Has a conversation about divorce or separation ever crept into my marriage? (It hasn't yet, but I'm on alert for it!)
3. Am I away from my kids for days on end?
4. Am I forgetting to create and design every day?

When you define your priorities alongside your deal breakers, you're building guard rails for your journey. This sets you up perfectly to frame your boundaries.

In effect, boundaries cut you off from anything that will distract you or keep you from achieving your goals. They keep you from entertaining things that make you spin in circles rather than fly ahead. A great place to start is by defining basic things like:

1. How many hours do you want to work per week?
2. Where do you want your work space to be?

3. How will you do your work?
4. When will you schedule meetings?
5. When won't you schedule meetings?

The list will steadily grow. But as you can see, when you start to set them, your life takes on a well-defined shape. Boundaries let your life flourish and grow, rather than wither and die of exhaustion!

However, boundaries have their sticky spots, too. One of the primary roadblocks I ran into after setting boundaries was communicating them well to family, friends, and clients. For example, there's a misconception that because I work from home, I can simply take breaks on a whim. Not even close. So I set firm boundaries by telling people, "I can't have lunch with you this week, but I can on the third Thursday of this month." or, "I can't serve on your committee until I've reached a 10 percent increase in sales."

At first, you may be scared to set boundaries like this. However, a magical thing happens when you do. People immediately respect you *and* your work more. Boundaries should be a major relief to you! No one is going to take you seriously if you're not striving for your best. And I don't believe for a second that your best is wearing the same yoga pants for three days, not showering, working a few hours a day, and snarking at your kids.

STAYING COMMITTED

Priorities and boundaries don't work when you don't commit to them. I define commitment as a pledge of action—a way of signing your name to execute on the plan, no matter what. And the key to staying committed is understanding your underlying "why"—the bottom-line reason you do what you do.

Whenever I'm challenged to remain committed, I know something has bumped into my "why" and rattled it. Your "why" helps you define how committed you are. And your level of commitment will speak volumes to others, whether or not you're serious about success.

When I get up at 5:15 a.m. and the day's workout includes 80 burpees, I may not want to do it. But I know I'll feel awesome, energized, and able to lift my toddler from her tantrum on the floor! I prioritize myself through exercise because I'm building myself into something better. I know where I'm going and why.

When our commitment is tested, it's a good thing. Every time it happens, it helps you see the reality of how seriously you're taking yourself. Let resistance to commitment light a fire in you. I still love it when people test my commitment to succeed. Every bag I sell proves the relevance and marketability of my mom's time-honored tradition. I love proving doubters wrong because, despite what they may say, I can build a successful business from home while raising a large family.

I can do this and pave the way for others. And the more people tell me it can't happen, the harder I drive to prove them wrong and lead other women to join me. Watch out world, here we come! Cue the super hero music and mic drop!

Question 1

Do you have defined priorities and boundaries?

Question 2

What are your roles in order of importance?

Question 3

What are your deal breakers?

Question 4

What is your answer right now for, "How is your business doing?"

Question 5

Deep down, why do you do what you do?

3

KEY DECISIONS

As moms, our days are jam-packed with decision making for everyone else. We live in a flurry of questions, details, and to-dos. As business owners, the same holds true. But as a mompreneur, I've learned there are six key decisions that, if you make well, make all the difference.

These key decisions set the stage for the entirety of your work. They outline the major elements that need a place in your business. The six decisions are:

1. When will you work?
2. Who will you work with?
3. Why do you do this work?
4. How will you work?

5. Where will you work?
6. What are your goals?

These decisions are critical to success because their answers frame out every working day. They are your "starting blocks." They hold you accountable to finish what you've set out to do. They act as parameters when you're stuck. And by making them in advance, you can minimize the overwhelming voice that yelps, "How are you possibly going to get everything done?!"

Just like me, you may have tiny, needy coworkers rolling, bouncing, and giggling around your house. They need their pants changed, clothes washed, and pacifiers rescued from the dog dish. So, unless you make the "big six" in advance, you'll struggle to gain momentum when you need it.

As you firmly answer these, you'll gain invaluable perspective. So the next time the jigsaw pieces of your life are scattered across the floor, you'll have a picture on the puzzle box as a guide. Your answers remind you what the masterpiece is supposed to look like.

MAKING YOUR KEY DECISIONS

In practice, this means if an action doesn't line up with your key decisions, it's not the right fit. So the big question is, how do you make them and then know you've gotten the answers right? That's what we're going to tackle in this chapter. To begin, let's talk about time.

Decision One: When Will You Work?

To decide when to work, determine the best hours in the day to block time. However, this time doesn't only need to be nap time or after lights out. Your children will adjust when they see you being disciplined about keeping set hours. Block out the hours you plan to do your best work. However, before you hop to it, think about how many hours are feasible, given your current life stage and business growth curve.

For example, I have three main work blocks each day: 8:30 to 11:30 a.m., 1:30 to 6 p.m., and then 8:30 to 9 p.m. For me, that's what works right now. But if you have a particularly busy season or start-up time, you may need more hours than I do. On the other hand, if you have a newborn, an 18-month old that destroys all things normal, are trying to teach your kiddos to use the "big potty," or your husband decided to build that deck, you may need to work less.

This decision isn't about putting an unrealistic burden on you. Instead, it's a way to measure what's possible this week. It's also a nice accountability measure. If you've blocked precious hours off to work, then you'd better not be scrolling Facebook or mopping floors!

Decision Two: Who Will You Work With?

After you decide when, you must ask yourself, "Who?" Here's the truth: *you're in denial if you think you can do this by yourself.* So, even if you're small right now, you need to decide who will work for and with you. Do you really think God would provide you with so much talent to spend your time working alone? No! He wants to bless others through you! I'm always the first person to tell people I don't do it alone. The products may have my name on it, but there are 20 unique sets of fingerprints on everything we do.

As you consider your team, I want you to think broadly. Don't limit this to employees right away. Instead, do you need childcare outside of the home a couple afternoons per week? Do you need a financial guru to go to work on your books? Do you need an office assistant, social media manager, or even another pair of hands to create?

Let your definition of "team" start large. Then, break it down to what makes financial and time-management sense for this stage of business. Think about all of the pieces you need to nestle together. Then work out who you need to bring to the table to make it all come together.

Decision Three: Why Do You Do This Work?

Next comes one of the biggest decisions of all, "Why do you do this work?" This answer needs to be buried as deep as your bones. What about your work motivates you to push through the hard times? What compels you to keep running when you're out of breath? Or, more importantly, what answer will ring true when you feel like you're failing as a mom, wife, and business owner?

Your real answer will blossom directly from *why* you started this business in the first place. But the truth is, if your "why" isn't deep enough, you'll fail every time. Your "why" is the ember. And if your ember goes out, you're not going to keep on sparking! It's something that grips you and gives you pause. It makes you reflect and retrace your reason for living right back to its source.

My "why" is simple. But to me, it's profound. I want to design and sew while I raise my babies from home. So I know anything that will steer me away from doing that will muddy my waters and dilute my purpose. In essence, your "why" is like a moral compass pointing true north. It signals why your work is a worthy ideal and reinforces the belief that you're equipped to execute on it.

For example, there are experts in my industry who'd say I'm crazy not to hire a giant mass producer to make my purses faster and cheaper. The underlying motive doesn't align with my "why," so it's an easy, "No thank you!" You see, any change in venue, and suddenly I'm not sewing from home with my babies. However, I can allow other women to help me from their homes while raising their families, too.

When you connect with the raw, gut-level reason you're in business, you've uncovered a time-tested tool. Your "why" will motivate you when you're overwhelmed. It will encourage you when you've had enough. And most of all, it will steer you true when you've lost your way.

Decision Four: How Will You Work?

After "why" comes "how." How are you going to do your work? This decision lays the bedrock for your business. It's a question that lines up the details and makes them march in order. But there are two basic areas you need to consider: sales and production.

Sales (AKA: How Will I Grow My Business?)

The first list of questions should get your sales juices flowing. Really, what you're asking is, "How will I grow my business?" This list could be endless, but here are some great starters:

- What marketing strategies will you use?
- What social media platforms should you be on?
- Will you knock on doors or rely on word of mouth?
- How many calls will you make and who will you call?
- Will you email 20 influencers?
- Will you sell in retail, online, at trunk shows, or fairs?

Production (AKA: How Will I Make the Stuff to Sell?)

The next set of questions deals with how you're going to deliver on what you're selling. Whether you offer products or services, you'll need to design a process for fulfilling sales. Here are some questions to begin:

- How much can you produce per week?
- How much of the work must you do yourself and what can you delegate?

- Do you need to design new products frequently? If so, how often?
- Will you sell/service locally, nationally, globally?

Decision Five: Where Will You Work?

I love this question because once you've defined a space, your dreams have a launch pad. And why not make it a pretty one? I'm in love with my "where." When you walk into my studio, you're surrounded by beautiful fabric (and work boots, Barbie dolls, and trucks rolling underfoot). You'll see inspirational wall coverings and photos of my "why" all over the place. On the long wall between my studio and my house, there is a large opening where you would normally see a door. Instead, we made an opening wide enough for the free flow of family and friends into my awesome "where."

I can't stress enough that this isn't a nicety. It's critical. If you don't have a "where," you're a work-from-home nomad. You travel from couch to toy room floor to kitchen counter—and sometimes all in the same morning. I promise it will be tough to get enough traction if you float around. But once you have a solid place that's "mommy's workspace," everyone—including yourself—will respect it. And with respect for the space comes honor for the work.

It doesn't need to be fancy; it simply needs *to be*. Find a closet and spruce it up with some wallpaper, a desk, and some goals. No matter where it is, start with something dedicated to all things work- and growth-related.

In the spirit of full disclosure, I'm 13 years in. And when you walk into my studio, you'll find more than fabric and inspiration. Open a drawer, and I guarantee you'll find loose Cheerios and dark chocolate. You'll find dolls underfoot, Barbies wrapped in fabric for naptime, and pictures askew from a flying ball or four. However, it's still my work space. And it's where I get it done.

Decision Six: What Are Your Goals?

Finally, you must ask yourself a question about "what." What are your goals? It's important to have your targets worked out. Otherwise, how do you know what success looks like, feels like, and if you're close or not?

If you begin by saying, "All I want is to have babies and make a couple of dollars," that's great! However, I'd counter with this: "How many dollars?" That's the problem with not setting goals—you never feel fully satisfied. You rob yourself of delicious "aha" moments. You're left without the satisfaction of making something out of nothing. You also forego the helpful (though not-so-warm-and-fuzzy) knowledge of what doesn't work. But you get a chance to rethink your plan.

You must have a goal to know whether or not you've succeeded. Otherwise, you're untethered. You don't have a clear measurement for growth. As the days wear on, this will become a motivation suck.

For instance, maybe you sold three plants today. Great, but was that your goal? If you didn't, how would you feel about three if it could have been five? Or, how would you feel if you were shooting for two? See the difference?

You should set a wide variety of goals as well. Some can be monetary; others may be networking-related. For instance, "I want to pass out 20 business cards today, and engage in 10 business-related conversations." Even if you bomb your first goal, you have a starting point for new ones. You also start answering needle-and-thread questions like, "If I'm going to pass out 20 cards, where am I going to do it?" In short, until you define what kind of "bag" you're going to make, you don't know how much thread to bring to the table.

You'll also discover patterns. For example, let's say for every three calls you make, you get one response. Then, as you increase to six calls a day, you get two. Bingo! How's that for motivation?

For me, I make a tally mark for every purse I plan to sell in a day. Every day I start fresh, and I keep the list out in front of me. Then, when I hit my goal, I have a happy dance party to celebrate with my coworkers. We blast Bruno Mars and wiggle like crazy people. It's a good thing our farmhouse is in the middle of nowhere, and you can't see my dancing!

Your goals can also be quirky, and totally you. At my shows, we have this under-the-radar rule. If we see four or more people with mullets, we know it's not our crowd. Also, if we're asked about fanny packs or see anything with a cat on it, it's time to bail! No matter your goals, quirky or serious, you need a benchmark from which to work.

OUTWORK YOUR FEAR

When the "goals" question comes up, I've noticed people can feel a bit scared. It's easy to worry that you'll set goals but never hit them. I often have the same fear. But I've internalized something that pushes me over the edge: I outwork my fear.

If I'm unsure of the outcome, I don't stare into the dark. I play out every scenario. Then I work out details so I'm ready for them all. Best case or worst case, I'm ready for what happens next. Outworking my fear means putting in the work to make it melt away. I take detailed notes for every event, every campaign, every product launch. This way, I can dissect what's working and what's not.

This also means I never do a show one time. I always try twice. I've learned the goal is never the problem—it's the effort and work-load leading up to game time. The part I can control is the hours I put in. I can always work harder. This also means never settling, even when things went your way.

If I hit a goal of selling out at a show, I immediately devise a plan to have an extra 70 bags cut to replace the inventory. If I only sell 15% of my goal, I work a plan to sell the rest via facebook or my own show. This is where fear fizzles away. Your brain loves to feed on excitement. It finds possibility delicious and always craves more.

THE REALITY OF EVERY BUSINESS OWNER

For goodness' sake, starting your own business comes with responsibility for days, problems for weeks, and fear piled on for years! But you *know* you're equipped when you answer that tiny punch in your gut to charge ahead. I remind myself I'm not the first person to have a certain problem. Instead I ask, "Who can I contact who's already leapt this hurdle?"

Finally, don't beat yourself up when fear creeps in. It's natural to doubt yourself. First, acknowledge it. Then ask, "Do I have more faith than fear?" While you may have doubts, don't feed them. Give them a nod of recognition, then work out ways to outwork them. Remember, you can sprint circles around your fear before it ever catches up to you. Now outwork it!

Question 1

Are there gaps of knowledge where fear is creeping into your mind?

Question 2

What resources can you use to fill those knowledge gaps?

Question 3

Which key decision are you most afraid of?

Question 4

Which key decision is easiest to make?

Question 5

What is your first key decision?

PART TWO

STRENGTHENING

4

HERE WE GO!

want to dig deeper into your goals. Because when I set my first ones, I was just trying to make ends meet. So I set the bar low because I didn't want to disappoint myself right out of the gate. After all, momentum is a precious commodity. What I soon learned, though, is low goals mean little output.

Goals attune your mindset. So when I verbalized, "I only need to make $100," I put a low ceiling on my attitude. Was that all I really wanted? Not by a long shot. So over time, I pushed myself. I got wild and inspired, deciding to accomplish ten times my original goal. I said, "I'm going to make $1,000!" Guess what happened? I only made $200. However, that was double what I made before. That's a win already!

The lie about goals is that showing up without them means you can't fail. But if you're thinking that way, it's likely because you don't expect to win. That was the truth for me. It means you'll focus on doing the minimum, rather than outworking your fear. Aim at nothing, hit nothing.

I'm a little notorious about this with my coaching clients. Whenever people tell me they haven't set any goals, I gently lay my hand on theirs, look them in the eyes, and ask, "How's that working out for you?" Spoiler alert: it's never going well!

ACTIONABLE ACCOUNTABILITY

I think of goals as actionable accountability. They give me the daily drive I need to spark momentum and rack up wins. I need them to remind myself there's a job to do, and this means more than peddling hope and posting inspirational quotes on Instagram. Goals are about hope—but they're also in place to plan for worst-case scenarios. Put another way, they give you the perspective to work *on* your business, and not simply *in* it.

The difference between a dream and a calling is the goals that power it. You pursue dreams because they're fun, they're exciting, and you're probably pretty good at whatever it is. However, calling is the worthy pursuit of purpose. It's about running toward what you're meant to do. And just like running, you'll set natural benchmarks. You'll pump your legs and look ahead, saying, "Okay, I need to make it to that tree... Now the top of this hill... Now across this river..." Pursuing purpose is action-oriented, and goals propel you forward.

In essence, you make something rather than hoping it shows up on your doorstep. After all, nobody who wants a baby sits around waiting for a stork to swoop in and drop off a bundled baby girl or boy. Making babies is another story for another book... and I won't be writing it! So right now, think about your purpose. Then, instead of saying, "My dream is to...", say, "I was created to..." Because creating is actionable—dreaming is not.

THE PLEASANT SIDE EFFECTS OF GOAL SETTING

As I assumed this mindset, my family started to get on board. Nothing is scarier than confiding in your circle of influence that you're quitting your job to build your own business. You feel raw and exposed. I know, because I remember those conversations well. I also know nothing gives you more drive than announcing it and putting yourself on the hook to prove you can do it. This goes for both yourself and the people who matter to you most.

Then, as you continue to talk about your specific goals, you have gentle, built-in accountability. You'll get asked, "So, are you getting close to doubling your revenue like you talked about?" The people who love you will check in so they can celebrate and cheer you on. I didn't used to share my goals because I worried people would judge me. Or worse yet, I would jinx myself. Instead, it's always done the opposite way.

When I imagine my life in an opposite scenario, with no goals in sight, I see a stressed-out mom who's totally overwhelmed. And worse yet, she's stuck in an aimless cycle wondering where to go from here. But because I have clarity on where I'm headed, I also feel the freedom to celebrate the outcome. When I hit big targets, it's time to buy the shoes or the red KitchenAid mixer—you know what I'm talking about!

"HERE WE GO!"

The phrase, "Here we go!" will be eternally stamped on my email signature. It's also something you'll hear if you spend any amount of time around me. It's become an affirmation and motivational phrase for me. When I say it, I imagine being on a roller coaster.

The brace swings down into your lap and you hear it lock in. Then you feel the tell-tale rattle and shake as the train of cars starts its ascent. You're looking straight into the air, heading right for the clouds themselves. You know what's coming and feel a mix of thrill, butterflies, and fear. But you simply can't wait for the free fall, the drop into madness. After all, it's why you came.

Crazy as it sounds, that's the feeling these words evoke in me. Just like standing in line for that exhilarating yet terrifying ride, there's the knowledge that you can back out. You can turn around and go back to an eight-to-five job. You can find a daycare, punch a clock, and attend yet another morning huddle. Or... you can stay in line.

I picture myself right at the crest of the first big drop, flinging my hands in the air and yelling, "HERE WE GO!" at the top of my lungs as I fall into empty air. I've decided I'd rather ride the roller coaster every day and experience the highs and lows, the joy and terror, than simply spin and bump along the lazy river. Attractive as they are, I'm not really into floaties. There's certainly a time and place for that. But for me, it's well after I've gotten my money's worth on the biggest ride I can find.

As a mompreneur, I encourage you to craft a similar mindset. It doesn't have to be a grand vision of roller coaster bliss. Instead, it needs to be something that resounds with your spirit. Are you a little wild? Are you driven and in control? Whatever makes you tick is the way your goals should direct you. And remember, even a roller coaster has seat belts, tracks, and safety tests galore (and barf bags)!

SETTING GOALS THE MOMPRENEUR WAY

When you set goals, start out with the boundaries you think your family and business can handle during your current life season. Make them reasonable so your work is sustainable. Honest to goodness, if you have toddlers and bedtime is like a high-stakes international negotiation, take that into account. Booking work, meetings, or shows from 6 to 10 p.m. five nights per week won't serve your family very well. But maybe you can swing one or two? Then, as your family falls into a routine, you can increase.

Personally, I can't be gone longer than four days at a time or mayhem ensues. I've learned day five is like the roller coaster flying off the tracks. So when I come home, there is so much physical and emotional cleanup, it's not worth it. Now, I set goals to only do art shows or conferences that last four days or less. I've found the burnout point for myself, my husband, and my kids.

Here are some telltale signs. If you arrive home and your kids are wearing each other's clothes and drinking from the same Sippy Cups you left with them, you're pushing it. Or even better, when you're catching up on laundry but your little boy only has two dirty pairs of undies and you've been gone a week, math is not adding up! You must interpret your family's system. But we'll talk more about that later.

You'll also notice your goals tie into the key decisions you made last chapter. For instance, to reach certain goals, you may need a superhero sidekick called a nanny or Super Granny. Trading kids for a few mornings or afternoons per week with a friend, neighbor, or family member may also offer some much-needed flexibility. You may even consider recruiting your cute and wonderful spouse after a few handshakes and some unspoken bargaining power.

The savvy mompreneur also sets visible goals. Write them down on a whiteboard or print them out. No matter how you do it, make them big and bold and tangible. Then you communicate your goals. So I may say, "Mommy is going to make 42 purses by Friday at 5 p.m." From there, my family can cheer me on as they watch the finished products stack up. A four-year-old will definitely help you remember your goals—trust me, they'll ask!

A MOMPRENEUR'S MARRIAGE

Communicating your goals to your kids is motivating, fun, and a great way to teach them how to work. It's also key to communicating (and agreeing) with your partner. Simply put, there is no person more important to have in your corner. Maybe you've had a conversation that's gone like this: "You want to quit your job? And do what? By yourself? And make *how* much money?"

It can be a hard sell. But when you have a plan laid out for your spouse to see, offer insight on, and ultimately buy into, you're much likelier to get there. This shows you're not simply meandering toward a dream. You're driving toward a better future for the family. If you know the data points that mark success, expectations are well-defined. This also gives them ammo to help you in tangible ways.

My husband and I have a running joke. When I ask him what he thinks my goals should be, he'll ask, "What did you sell last year at this time?"

And if I reply, "45 bags."

He'll say, "Alright, sell 60!"

I'll counter, "52."

He'll say, "Deal!"

It may seem like a simple exchange. But because he's bought in, it's extremely encouraging to me. Side note, did you notice his goal was bigger than mine? Your spouse wants success for you!

THE ROADMAP

My husband's support means he believes that my skills and work ethic can attain the goals we talk about. But there's a delicate dance a mompreneur needs to have with her goals. It's easy to get amped up on your goals and aim for the stars. As I described earlier, this can be a good thing sometimes. However, there are sticky spots to avoid as well.

Make sure every goal has an action plan. If a particular goal is lofty and aggressive, you need to have a map to know how you're going to get there. If you can't sketch out a plan, you're in dangerous waters. Your plan should be broken into weekly and daily action steps. Be like a thermometer, knowing exactly what the temperature is as you progress. This way, you know if you need to narrow your goals for a particular season.

This doesn't mean you need to know the future. No one but God gets to know every detail! However, you should have a measurable plan that you can adjust along the way. I've found when this isn't in place, it's easy to simply work, work, work without a clear direction. And while you feel like you're doing things, you may not be doing the *right* things. None of us has time for wasted effort.

This is another area where the right team is invaluable. Advisors who have been where you're going or coaches to walk with you along the way can make all the difference. The right ones help you think critically and see pitfalls lurking in your blind spots. We all have them. So recruit the right insight to help you execute with as few stumbles as possible. However, don't take advice from people you wouldn't trade places with.

THE SATISFACTION TEST

In addition to advisors, coaches, mentors, and the rest, I also employ a simple visualization technique. I picture myself as vividly as possible having achieved a certain goal. Then, I dwell there and explore my level of satisfaction. Your mind is a wonderful tool, and this allows you to use it in a powerful way.

Hitting a goal feels fantastic. It's like a perfect strike; all the pins get blown away. Other times, however, there's more cost than benefit to achieving something. Maybe you have accomplished something big, but your family ends up an emotional wreck. Is plowing through resistance at all costs like a freight train the right path here? Maybe... but maybe not. While it may not be a perfect way to measure future satisfaction, it is close.

PREVENTING OVERWHELM
BY TRACKABILITY

When you've determined whether or not a goal is worth the blood, sweat, and tears, you also need to combat "goal overwhelm." While a goal may be extremely satisfying and merits the cost to achieve, it doesn't mean it won't feel overwhelming. This was one of my biggest hurdles when I first set goals.

To begin, keep your list lean. Start with three or four goals. Keep them simple, concise, and 100 percent trackable. Then, as you progress, take copious notes. You don't need anything fancy here. I just use a legal pad for all my note-taking madness.

Today, a key part of my goal-setting process is studying past projects. This way, I have basic facts to start with. For me, a good rule of thumb is to add at least 10 percent to what I previously achieved. However, if you don't have a data set to work from, take an educated guess. At least estimate realistic numbers to work from. But there's a nifty trick for that, too.

Let's imagine you're about to do your first house show selling a product. Think about what you're going to do, and ask yourself this question: "Am I the first person who's ever sold at a house show before?" The answer is obviously a big, "No!" You're rarely reinventing the wheel. So, think about similar business models or industries to yours. Then, track some experienced people down and have some conversations.

For me, this a go-to example because it's exactly what I did. I called a well-known Mary Kay gal who'd been in business for 30 years. I asked if I could buy her coffee and ask her questions. She agreed, and I came prepared with a list. I learned so many things. But most of all, I gained some practical data points to work from.

I knew my goal was to sell 10 to 12 pieces. So, I asked her how many people I needed to get to attend. I learned that average direct-sales company shows see about 30 percent of those invited attend. And then 50 percent of those in attendance will buy. After some quick math, I realized that to meet my goal, I needed to invite about 100 people. This would mean about 30 would come, and 15 would buy. And I gleaned this all from a cup of coffee!

I also contacted my local small business administration office and then followed up with all of the resources they gave me. Simply put, mompreneurs can't afford to waste any time, money, or energy pursuing the wrong paths. We need to find the most efficient, proven methods of success. And to do that, we often need to look outside of ourselves.

WHAT'S NEXT?

As you can tell, I love goals and would never dream of running a business without them. Though there are many more tips and tricks to share, these are excellent starting points for you. I hope you feel energized and have experienced clarity here. If you're looking for more, I also host *The Encourager* podcast for mompreneurs and get even further into the nitty-gritty.[1]

The bottom line, though, is achieving big goals requires hard work. Business books, magazines, and the internet are littered with people touting Instagram lifestyles of total freedom and ease that accompanies being your own boss. But freedom comes at a cost—a cost no one but you are responsible for paying. There's no safety net, no one else to take up the slack if you decide not to put in the effort each day.

Surrounding every successful mompreneur is a circus, rather than a life filled with sipping lattés and having fun lunch dates. Each day is your gift with which to work. What you do with every second adds up, and you are 100 percent responsible for the results. In a word, freedom equals responsibility. However, my podcast is called *The Encourager*, after all. So let's end on a bright note.

Take this opportunity to reframe failure. My career is filled with slipping on the sticky spots and tripping into the classic pitfalls I alluded to. But when I don't reach my goals, I don't beat myself up. Instead, my first thought is, "What can I learn from this?" Failure is

---

[1]You can find all series and episodes at https://shoprsd.com/the-encourager-podcast/

simply a curve in the road. It may be a deviation from the path, but it's certainly no stop sign.

Success is a cocktail of smart goals, hard work, and lots of grace— for your team, your tiny coworkers, and also yourself. My mindset is certainly that failure is not an option. But you're in the driver's seat. You define failure. The only time I fail is when I don't learn how to to be better.

As you work and learn and live, don't forget to celebrate. So I'll let you in on a little secret. If this book is as well-received as I want it to be—the red KitchenAid mixer is mine!

Question 1

Why would you hire you (or fire you)?

Question 2

What will be your first realistic goal?

Question 3

What will be your first aggressive goal?

Question 4

In what area do you need advisors and accountability—
and from who? (Shameless plug: I offer coaching!)

Question 5

How will you celebrate? (I suggest Rebekah Scott
bags, shoes, and KitchenAid appliances!)

5

HOW YOU WILL MAKE MONEY

f you flipped through the book and this is the first chapter you're reading, I totally get it. Making money is a sweet-spot topic for me, too. Let's be real, it's a major part of why we're in business. So, if you're a husband, an aspiring mompreneur, or anyone dipping their toes in the water to see if this book is legit, let me give you a snapshot of my resume.

I'm a mom of four, a happily married wife, and have been in business for 13 years. If the classic 10,000-hour rule makes you an expert, then I qualify as a seamstress, business coach, mompreneur, laundry ninja, diaper changer, and casserole maker. And my only objective is to help you (or your spouse) succeed! So let's jump into the deep end of your business and clarify your path to cash.

WHAT IS A BUSINESS MODEL?

When I started my business, someone told me, "You absolutely *must* have a business model." So, after a quick Google search, I downloaded a business model template and filled it out. I mostly B.S.-ed my way through it. But it was done, so I checked it off my list and promptly forgot about it.

It sat in a drawer, collecting dust, and was irrelevant to my day-to-day business. I didn't understand the value—or practicality—of a solid business model. A business model is simply a framework for how you will make make money. It outlines the avenues you're going to pursue to bring in the dollars.

The first model I filled out led me to believe it needed to be a complicated, clinical dissection of technical jargon. It felt like a document to hand over to bankers so you can get a loan and look respectable. However, I've experienced firsthand that it's much more valuable than that.

After three years in business, I wasn't making ends meet. I was working really hard, but mostly spinning in place. I had to reevaluate what I was doing and how I was doing it. In essence, I needed a business model that functioned in the real marketplace; not a plan to appease a man in a suit.

So I chucked out the old one and charted a fresh course. I asked myself one big question: "How do I intend to make money over the next three years?" From there, the rest of the dots fell into place. The intimidation evaporated and I had an energizing clarity. And even better, this model was only a page long—and it worked. Plus, I did end up submitting this one to a "man in a suit" (actually, a girl in a cute pair of red Jimmy Choos) who worked at the small business bureau. She helped me iron out a few shortcomings and provided helpful feedback.

TRUNK SHOWS WERE MY JAM!

This first plan consisted of just five questions:

1. Why am I in business?
2. What are my talents?
3. What are my one-, five-, and 10-year goals?
4. What ways will money flow in?
5. What ways will money flow out?

At first, my model was extremely fluid and I discovered that trunk shows were my jam! I made money, gained valuable experience, and gained important traction with customers.

Then, I branched out and began traveling four to six times per month. These shows were steadily profitable and also increased my name recognition. From there, the path to selling in retail and online emerged. Obviously, the more revenue streams I secured, the more secure my business became. And the decision-making clarity I needed stemmed directly from a well-defined business model. Rather than a straitjacket, it was a vehicle for growth.

The best part was, it didn't need to be a ten-page report—just a straightforward plan for growth, cash flow, and direction.

EARNING YOUR FIRST DOLLARS

Before I penned my first business plan, my life as an entrepreneur began in fourth grade. I was an eager seamstress and loved making fleece joker-style stocking caps. In a stroke of genius, I decided to try my hand at sales between the monkey bars and tire swing. My first transactions came from three classmates: Jan, David, and Jodi. I sold them for $5, and I couldn't believe my fortune. I'd made $15 in a single day. *My hats—they liked MY hats!*

The light bulb had turned on and I was off to the sewing machine to launch a new line of boxers—though I could never get my mom to agree to letting me sell those on the playground. However, I quickly discovered a slight flaw in my business model. I sold my hats for $5, but they cost me $7 to make. I was losing money. Being the wonderful woman she is, my mom helped me do the math. I was determined to make money, so it was time to raise my prices. My first dollars also taught me my first lesson in cash flow and business models.

Fast forward to when I started Rebekah Scott Designs, and this cash flow lesson stuck with me. There's a misconception that you need money to make money—but it's so not true! I had limited money to invest in fabric, so I dug through the remnant bins at department stores to find discounted materials. It was creativity—not cash—that got me started. I grew rich with the currency of creativity. Then came my next hurdle.

I sold through every purse I made, which was great. But I still didn't have enough money to invest in a stockpile of fabric. I set to pacing (which is how I do my best scheming) and then had an epiphany.

"I do have really cute curtains..." I said.

I grabbed a stool and cut them up into adorable, one-of-a-kind purses and kept the funds rolling in. I made enough money to buy more fabric and keep creating. To make my first few dollars, I capitalized on low-cost opportunities.

From the outset, I was determined not to rely on a line of credit. So I had to think outside the box to market my goods. To get some steam, I applied to every little town fair I could find within a 75-mile radius. These booths only cost between $10 and $20, and allowed me to raise awareness and carve out my niche.

If you were there, you would have seen a momma handing out over 50 business cards per day with a kid in a sunhat, stroller, and slathered in sunscreen smiling beside me. I didn't sell much at these fairs, but I reached my goals of making connections. Slowly, I built a sales network outside of my immediate friends and family.

At this stage, I knew it was time for a website—but within reason. You don't need to invest $50,000 right out of the gate (though eventually you may). I hit the pavement searching for a web designer in my price range. And low and behold, I knocked and the door was opened (see Matthew 7:7). I found a girl in the same boat who was scaling up her business. And just like a 19th-century hunter trading pelts for goods, I traded purses for a website!

I learned that before you move to the next level, you need to be able to sell the little you have to work with. If you can't move what you've got now, how are you going to sell when you have a lot?

MISTAKES ALONG THE WAY

Though I made some smart moves early on, I also had some disasters. For instance, because I didn't do my usual thorough research, I made a $10,000 investment in a sales catalog that absolutely flopped. Over time, I learned to keep investing in my website. And today, it's my main source of monthly sales.

That investment has continually proven a wise one. I made it because I learned to ask questions of my customers first. Not only will you learn from your customers, but they'll direct you to what they want. Listen to the people with the dollars in order to make savvy decisions with your own money. Identify your lowest hanging fruit (think chopping up your curtains) and start lean. Then listen, listen, listen to your customers. They'll help point you toward reality.

THE NUMBERS YOU NEED TO KNOW: COGS, TOGS, AND WHAT TO CHARGE

Just like 4th-grade Rebekah learned, you need to make more money than you spend. Though you may reply, "Duh!" It's not always so obvious.

Cost of Goods Sold

In business vernacular, you need to know your cost of goods sold (COGS) before you can understand anything else. Unless you know, to the penny, how much your products or services cost, you're simply guessing. Knowing these numbers are what set the experts apart from the hobbyists. Pros know their nickels; amateurs go with their gut. Here's an example of how I dissect my COGS on one of my products, the *Elizabeth* bag (which, I might add, is beautiful and so darn handy). I calculate the cost of each of the following.

Anatomy of the Elizabeth Bag

- Two D-rings
- One hook
- Two zippers
- Two elbows
- One base
- Two long handles
- One zipper pull
- 2.5 yards of lining fabric
- 1.5 yards of outside fabric
- 1.5 yards interfacing fabric
- The hard cost of labor for one outside seamstress, and one inside seamstress
- The hard cost of labor for me to finish the bag
- Shipping, if applicable
- Booth, tradeshow, and travel costs
- Taxes (state and federal)
- Handling fees

It's key for me to know my numbers because I work on razor-thin margins compared to competing purse companies. My model involves work-from-home mommies and they cost more because they are worth more!

After detailing the COGS for each of my products, I was able to calculate the margin I needed to stay in business. Even though my margin is much slimmer because I employ work-from-home moms rather than outsourcing to a mass producer, I've been able to make it work. I realize the price you need to charge and what you are comfortable with are giants to wrestle. However, study your industry. Also, consider therapy to discuss and explore your own self-worth. I've personally found this to be very helpful.

Time of Goods Sold

Your COGS is closely related to your time of goods sold (TOGS). When are the peak times of year your product or service sells well? Or on a smaller scale, do you notice a more effective day of the week to sell?

After studying our social media data, the analytics point to Thursday nights as a hot night for us. So we capitalize on that—not just to make more money, but to better offer our customers want when they want it. Nailing the timing means you're serving your customers best.

How to Price Your Products and Services

Finally, after you know your COGS and TOGS, you can work on a competitive analysis. Or put another way, you can figure out how to best price your wares. There are two pitfalls here:

1. Pricing yourself too high, and out of competition.
2. Pricing yourself too low, degrading your market and undervaluing yourself.

In the beginning, an expert advisor told me you want people to think of you as the standard of excellence. This means pricing and branding yourself as the market leader. For me, I knew I had to deliver on two things to nail this: quality and customer service. Every social media post, email, and stitch needed to overflow with those standards. This way, I knew people would say, "She is worth every penny."

For instance, if you're a photographer who charges $50 per session, your customer assumes you're only worth $50. However, if you charge $150, you're in line with 80 percent of professional photographers in the area.

OVERCOMING NUMBER PHOBIA

In the beginning, I was scared of setting dollar amounts. I didn't want to overprice myself and never sell anything. But I also believed my work had real value. So I learned a simple trick that helped me overcome my number phobia.

Instead of looking at my numbers as hard dollars (e.g. "This purse costs $140."), I began referring to dollars as "points". So instead of shifting dollar signs, I was playing with numbers I could move around. I treated them like a scoreboard. So when the numbers were positive, I was winning. And when they weren't, I was losing. All I had to do was stay ahead, and I would keep winning. My mindset and lingo became:

- 14 points need to go to fabric.
- 2 points need to go to the label.
- 6.5 points need to go to the tax man.
- 6 points need to go for shipping.
- Don't forget the points for the home team!

Don't be intimidated by business models or numbers. Being a mompreneur is hard work—there's no mincing words here. But it's a worthy pursuit and totally doable. To this day, I take comfort in knowing there is nothing new under the sun. There is always a model, process, method, or system I can learn to help me grow. I can always shape and reframe it for my needs. I don't have to reinvent the wheel to keep my business rolling—and neither do you.

Question 1

How will you make money? (e.g., What kind of hats
are you going to sell on the playground?)

Question 2

How much will it cost you to make your hats? (COGS)

Question 3

How will customers get to you and how will you get to them?

Question 4

Will you have peak seasons? (TOGS)

Question 5

Make a one-page business model with at least two questions answered: "How will the money come in?" and "How will the money go out?"

PART THREE

ACCELERATING

6

YOUR SUPER SKILL

N ow it's time to rummage through your closet and pull out your superhero cape. We're about to talk super skills. Your super skill is the thing you can do at breakneck speeds, with high attention to detail, and feel on top of the world while doing it!

You sing, laugh, fly, and dominate in this area. It's something you can do for hours on end without even realizing hours have passed by. This is the sweet spot where you're in the zone the whole time. And then, once finished, you're not exhausted—you're energized.

As you grow as a mompreneur, you're going to face the hurdles of both family life and business. This means your team will grow, and you may even add another little coworker or two! But you must always own your super skill and hold it tight. It's the thing that no one can do like you can, and something you should never hire out all the way. In fact, if you keep at it, your super skill will actually ener-gize you to maintain and grow your business.

So, the weighted question is: *What's your super skill?*

MY SUPER SKILL

Resist the urge to overcomplicate this. Your super skill can be a simple, everyday task. The important thing is to absolutely own it and keep it up all day. For example, my super skill is mass production (odd as it may sound). I can do it day-in and day-out without ever feeling exhausted. In fact, I've done it for 13 years now.

Here's what it looks like in my life. Every time I think of a new project or item to introduce, my thoughts immediately focus on how to mass-produce it. I instantly calculate how many cuts it will take and what kinds of fabrics I need to serge (a serger is a souped-up four-threaded sewing machine). I imagine big piles of material just waiting to be crafted. I outline what the kits I hand out to my seam-stresses will look like. Honest to goodness, I love everything about mass-producing. So even though I've hired other work-from-home moms to help, I still do the serging and make the kits to this day. This means I handle about 3,000 pieces in a single kit-building day—and I love every second of it.

I realized mass production was my super skill when my business experienced a spike in growth and I hired some help. The parts I was most hesitant to give away or train someone else to do were the things I loved. Also, the truth was that no one could even touch my speed.

I had built on so much experience because of the hours involved in mass production—I simply knew it better. I had no problem hiring out things I didn't excel at, like taxes and Facebook. But I found out that maintaining this part of production was essential to both my business and my enjoyment.

Your super skill doesn't have to be sexy or cool. In fact, for most of us, it won't be. After all, you probably weren't expecting the phrases "mass production" and "super skill" to be used in the same sentence. Mass producing isn't romantic, heroic, or sexy—but it's mine.

This realization changed my life and business. I knew which areas I could hire out so that I could focus on honing my unique skill set. This meant I could focus on doubling (or even tripling) our output without sacrificing quality. I also knew if I used my super skill each week, I'd stay happy and energized.

Your super skill is usually a unique—even offbeat—thing. It will flood every part of your life too. Once you identify it, you'll notice you use it all the time. I don't simply mass-produce purses—I mass-produce *everything*. I don't make one casserole, I multiply the recipe and freeze the rest. I don't make make 10 pillow backs, I fold and cut 20. It's a compulsion as much as a conscious choice. It's just how I'm wired.

TIME TO ACCELERATE

To find your super skill, I've built a simple tool for you. There are three facets of yourself that your super skill will touch: *joy, skills, and compulsion.* Think about each of them as a personal question like the following:

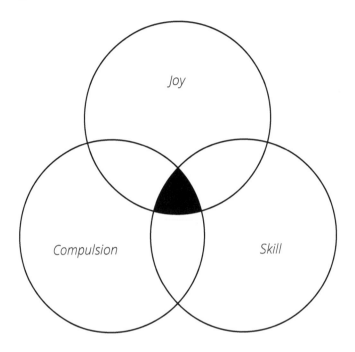

1. <u>Joy:</u> What can you do non-stop? What activity gives you more energy back than you put in?
2. <u>Skills:</u> What are you naturally good at? What were you doing at the age of four?
3. <u>Compulsion:</u> What are you always itching to do? What do you love to do and need so much it's actually creepy?

Your super skill is where these three converge. And once you've found it, break out the superhero cape and let's fly!

Once you've determined what your unique skill is, make sure you block off your calendar to use it every day. The more you improve yourself in this area, the faster you'll accelerate your business's growth. For example, a key part of my mass production is serging. In fact, my serger was a gift I got for graduating college. Some people get cars and cry; I got a serger and cried (thanks Mom and Dad!).

As I improved, I realized an industrial serger could increase my efficiency. After some intense research, I determined an industrial machine would shave 23 seconds off of each piece. This would mean I could serge 2,000 pieces in two hours instead of four. This is where my super skill gets creepy!

Notice how keeping this skill doubled my productivity and output? Yours will do the same for your business. But that will only happen if you work it from every angle. How can you do it more efficiently *and* effectively? In my mind, I measure my performance by whatever will improve my quality and customer service.

DESIRING MASTERY

There is something to be said when you are a true master of a skill. I love when people ask me how I do what I do because, in a way, I look superhuman (cue the cape blowing in the wind). However, this is only because I've mastered a key area of my workflow rather than being a generalist in everything. The same is true of you!

As you increase in mastery, you'll also experience greater fulfillment in the work you produce. When other people see your joy and output, it raises everyone's perception of your work. It also inspires them to push harder and accomplish more. This only comes from finding the process or skill God uniquely equipped you to do. This isn't about hustle. We don't need to push harder or accomplish more—just hone our super skill.

Right now, you have all of the skill sets you need. Your problem isn't knowledge, it's simply execution. You have every tool for your super skill right now. It's simply time to execute on them. In my life, this is where my work has become a way for me to worship God. What will it look like for you?

"WE'RE NAILING IT, BEV!"

You will be heroic. Time will melt away and you'll experience so much attuned energy, it'll be frightening. Your level of concentration will outmatch a magnifying glass and sunbeam! How do I know? Because sometimes my machine literally smokes, I'm moving so fast. My satisfaction is at an all-time high when I see the spool of thread on my serger rapidly disappear.

Naturally, I have a great relationship with my serger and affectionately named her Beverly. So, whenever we're moving at lightspeed, I'll exclaim, "We're nailing it, Bev!" So, dive deep into your super skill, achieve greater mastery, and find your Bev.

Now, it's time to add a logo your cape! Next up, theme music.

Question 1

What were you doing the last time
you completely lost track of time?

Question 2

What were you doing at age four?

Question 3

If people were to say, "That's so [your name]!"

What would they be referring to?

Question 4

What can't you keep yourself from doing?

Question 5

Where do your joy, skill, and compulsion converge?

7

WORK YOUR SYSTEMS

t may not be fun or even thrilling, but I talk about systems *a lot*. The reason is because without them, I wouldn't be where I am today. In truth, I'd probably be back in the same spot I was in the opening story. I'd be cradling my crying little boy, carting three others behind me, bawling my eyes out, and canceling art shows because I'm in over my head. Those moments on the floor in the fetal position changed me, though! That was the precise moment I decided I needed to build systems to make sure this scene never repeated itself.

When I talk about systems, I mean a group of similar methods that work together to make your work week as productive as possible. The systems I've created are designed to touch every role in your life, and then help them sing in beautiful harmony. Their goal is to help you account for your roles each day and meet them to the best of your ability. So in this final chapter, I'm going to share the four foundational systems I've put in place in my own life and business.

YOUR FOUNDATIONAL SYSTEMS

I created four systems because my life is divided into four major roles. My kiddos have to eat—that's a food system. I have to work to feed them—that's a work system. They need a joyful momma—that's a "me" system. And of course, I have to spend time with them—that's a family system.

These four systems combine forces to keep everyone fed, clothed, loved, and cuddled. And just as important, I keep my joy while the rodeo surges on. Keeping your food, family, work, and "you" plates spinning requires an incredible amount of energy and time. However, when you synchronize them and ensure everything has its place, you're in the sweet spot.

When I started, however, it certainly didn't look synchronized. There was a lot of chaos to rein in. So I started from this premise: if I can take care of myself and control my actions, emotions, and thoughts, I can take care of everyone else that much better.

The first system I successfully implemented was the "me" system, and that meant waking up early to exercise. I freed my body from bad toxins, got a good sweat going, and thought more clearly. It's certainly cheaper than therapy and alcohol! It also gave me a quiet space to pray, read my Bible, and set my spirit up for success.

This absolutely revolutionized my life, and it will do the same for you. I intentionally put this system first because it's automatically the one moms put last. The moment it clicks and you're healthier, mentally clearer, more emotionally stable, and just plain happier, everything else can fall into place.

Your "Me" System

First, understand that your "me" system doesn't necessarily mean you'll be alone. Before kids, I loved Cherry Coke, bubble baths, and *People* Magazine. But today, I settle for juice boxes, dirty dishwater, and Dr. Seuss. Ah, motherhood! Obviously, our little coworkers are going to be around us a lot. Your "me" system isn't about changing that.

My kids can be with me, but I'm still doing my thing. It's a mindset shift. It's an action plan that ensures your needs are met first so you can better meet the needs of your family, team, and work. This is the path to working fully charged rather than on blinking red bars. Just like your cellphone, if you're running at 35 percent, you'll never make it through the day.

For me, this means I'm up before the kiddos and I prioritize exercise as the first order of the day. The beautiful circus is about to begin and those cute little acrobats are about to whack you in the face. So even if your exercise of choice is walking—break a sweat and get it done!

Then, I spend time with God and say aloud my actionable affirmations. Every morning, I affirm:

- I will have joy as I raise my children.
- I have all the tools I need to execute on the gifts and roles God has given me.
- I will outwork my fear.
- I treat my customers with utmost respect.
- My employees trust my leadership skills.
- I will exercise grace in its various forms (1 Peter 4:10).

Those affirmations, along with some others, have become powerful anchors for my mind. Regardless of how you start or what you say, the "me" system is about taking great care of yourself so you are at your best for everyone else.

Your "Food" System

After I'd gotten into my "me" system groove, I took the next logical step. I made a food system. We waste an incredible amount of mental bandwidth thinking, "What am I going to feed everyone for supper?" When I recognized this, I made a pact with myself. All of my food choices for the day would be made by 7:30 a.m. That means lunch, snack, and supper are planned every morning.

Not only does that free up mental space, it also frees up time. We spend so much time preparing food. So if you make your decisions in advance, you can shop, prep, and eat on schedule. This system is simple but majorly effective. It doesn't have to be rocket science. But you do need a system.[2]

Your "Family" System

When you find a rhythm for the first two systems, you'll have more capacity for the third one: your family system. It answers the

---

[2]If you want more practical tips for implementing a food system, my podcast, *The Encourager*, is a great place to start! I cover this topic extensively.

question, "What does a successful family life look like to you?" Does it mean a solid three hours of quality time every day—or five because of your current life stage? Will you have date nights with your spouse? If so, how often?

Essentially, the purpose of this system is to know your family's priorities so you can work to meet them first. For my husband and me, this all started with a conversation about the three things we want our kids to know by the time they're 18. Obviously, there are thousands of things we hope they know. But we've whittled the list down to three characteristics we want to describe them as: kind, honest, and humble. So we emblazoned a handmade family crest with our family name and these qualities on our kitchen door (though the crest does look a bit like a pregnant pig!). Everything we do and teach them revolves around instilling those values.

It's also helpful for your family system to include areas of family recreation. Simply put, what's your family's jam? Are you campers? Are you pool people? Rodeo goers? Boxers? Lego ninjas? What does family fun time look like and how will you nestle it in amongst everything else?

As you can see, all of your family priorities will fall into place as you prioritize them. The key part of the system is to get started and revise along the way!

Your "Work" System

Now that you've taken care of yourself, everyone is full and happy, and your family has the time it needs—you can *really* get to work.

The work system defines the boundaries for your weekly working time in relation to the other systems. This is the way you're going to stay accountable to achieving your goals and building a successful business.

In reality, the bulk of this book has been about how to set up a work system. From making key decisions to setting goals to your business model, we've covered a lot of ground. For mompreneurs, though, what's most important is they find a life rhythm that doesn't require sacrificing any systems at the expense of another. Your work system is no different.

You don't have to become strangers to your kids to build a successful business. But you also don't have to run around in well-worn yoga pants without showering to be a successful momma. The work system is where you treat your business with the respect and integrity it deserves. It is so valuable—and that's why you dedicate a system to it. When you do, you get to tie on your cape and take flight with your super skill!

IMPLEMENTING YOUR SYSTEMS

Throughout this book, I've given scores of examples and suggestions. And right now, I hope your mind is teeming with ideas and inspiration (I know mine is!). If you don't have any systems right now, however, just focus on one. Start with your "me" system first because it's the easiest and least time-consuming. Plus, let's get real... If I didn't ask you to put it first, you would have put it last. I know you!

Now, commit to at least 10 days of true effort. As your business and family grow, so must you. So prioritize yourself. Imagine yourself as a tree and your "me" system as the roots. If a tree is going to grow, spreading its branches high and wide, it must dig deeper roots as it does. After all, a massive tree with shallow roots is soon called a log!

As you build your life systems, you'll be astounded how much life begins to look like the way you'd always dreamt it could. And as you continue on this journey, you'll break through barrier after barrier. Your mindset will change, because you'll realize how much you can actually accomplish. You will change your life through action.

When the fears, doubts, and anxieties come, outwork them. We gain momentum through action, not feelings and thoughts. There is validity to therapy and counseling, and I encourage you to seek them out if you need it. For now, though, what are you going to do to get your systems running in harmony and take over the world? Whatever it is, it's going to work. Because, like I've been saying, you're already equipped to execute!

Question 1

What are three things you can do for your "me" system at your current life stage (i.e., read a devotional, run, and pray)?

Question 2

What actionable affirmations will you write
and recite? (Feel free to wear your cape.)

Question 3

For your food system, where and
when will you shop, prep, and make?

Question 4

What is your family crest? What three qualities do you
want your kids to embody by the time they're 18?

Question 5

Where and when will you do your work each day?

(See Chapter Three.)

CONCLUSION

For years now, I've been passionate about helping mompreneurs grow. Two years ago, I set out to write this book and help as many as I could on their journeys. But when I weighed the cost of writing such an important book with the stages of my family and business, I knew there wasn't room to do everything well. I was ten months pregnant with Miss Pixyn, and God had sent me on a 20-percent growth curve.

So I waited.

But guess what? You're holding my book in your hands right now!

I want to encourage you that sustainable growth takes time. As of now, I've been at this for 13 years and I still have much learning, growing, and supervillain-fighting to do. But I wouldn't trade any one of those years for the world. I may have grown it small, but the intentions were large. Because, all told, they are how I got to be the woman I am today. They are the reason I run my business, love my husband, nourish my kiddos, and value myself the ways I do.

So if I've succeeded in this book, you should see a clear path ahead. I realize the path is full of obstacles to jump over, dodge, and chase, but you should feel charged and energized. And your mindset should be one that's looking long-term. You know you're equipped to execute. God has given you every tool you will need to do this. God has equipped you with a unique super skill. You have every tool and ability you need to do great things.

I also realize this is a lot to take in, especially when you have an already full life. But treat this book like an application for your dream job—the job you created. This is a job where you are fulfilled in every role, and are the leader you know you can be. All this requires is action, which I know you can handle. After all, you bought this book.

So I encourage you to trust yourself and the systems you create. Trust that if you fulfill your roles every morning, afternoon, and night, you'll build a life that continually astounds you. You'll wake up in the dark morning hours, look around, and say, "I knew it could be this good." And then the kiddo-powered alarm clock will go off early, signaling that another day of the beautiful circus has begun.

But then you'll smile, list out five things you're grateful for, tuck your cape in, tie on your running shoes, and go pull out the meat you defrosted the night before. That's right, you got this.

ABOUT THE AUTHOR

I am an original seed company. I have loved sewing since I was four years old—kneeling next to mom and begging her to let me cut some scraps of fabrics to create something on my own. Until she allowed me to belly up next to her sewing machine, I would take Kleenexes and a stapler and create things for my Barbie. Eventually Mom decided I did in fact have what it took to honor this tradition and handed the baton over to allow me to sew and design.

I started Rebekah Scott Designs in 2003. I wanted to have children and be able to stay at home to raise them by my side and design with them close. I knew I had to start a business somehow—so my husband and I worked hard to become debt free with the Dave Ramsey program and eventually my hubby (seeing the itching that went on all over me when I needed to sew!) said, "OK—launch your business!" And LAUNCH I did! The first night I stayed up till 2 a.m. sewing in my happy place, humming and thanking God for the opportunity to see my seeds grow.

In the beginning I had a dry spell—so I improvised. I knew I needed fabric to sell some purses but didn't have any cash flow, so I paced around thinking of various solutions and one thought came to mind—I have really cute curtains! So there I was cutting my curtains into adorable handbags!

Phone: 605.951.6244
Facebook.com/ShopRSD
Podcast: The Encourager
Facebook.com/EncouragerPodcast
Email: info@shoprsd.com

Each year the seeds took on new sprouts—new employees to make things faster, better, and be able to harvest more fruit and different varieties for the new customers. We employ South Dakota women eager to work and sow good seeds in a growing America. With good water, plenty of help, and continued support from good roots—Rebekah Scott Designs became a federally trademarked direct sales brand.

I can't emphasize enough how much I love what I have grown all these years. We have four little ones watching close by. They continue to inspire me, put smiles on my heart, remind me the whole reason I "grew such a large garden," and allow me grace to balance all the roles I have been blessed with.

Enjoy the fruits of my labor! They are made with love, determination, good rain, and plenty of sunshine! Rejoice!

equippedtoexecute.com